Acknowledging LOSS

Praise for
Amarendra Khatua's Work

Amarendra's Poems mix memories with haunting words and etch superb pictures of love and despair, waiting and melancholia'.
– **Graciela Aroaoz**, Poet and president, Argentina Writers Association

Khatua's Acknowledging Loss *epitomises the dynamic lifetime of a poet/bureaucrat who has now delved deeper into the forest of silence to create poems of inconceivable heights, a castle of cravings inside the forest of his lonely bones where "heart asks simple questions/And body will seek sinful offerings." Here the poet's fingers grow feathers and love oozes out of his each pore to conjure up these brilliant ruminations on life, loss and regeneration. A splendid feat of imagination."*
– **Yuyutsu Sharma,** Himalayan Poet & Author of *Annapurna Poems* & *A Blizzard in my Bones: New York Poems*

Agony of losing in love, seeking definition of eternal waiting and defining depths of human relationship in well- crafted imagery – Amarendra's Poem resembles the familiar tradition imposed by Neruda's tradition'.
– **Juany Rojas**, Poet, Chile

Vivid Portrayal of love and longing, exile and waiting.
– **Jorge Paolantonio,** Poet & Novelist, Argentina

In Amarendra's magical précis of words, corralling disparate emotions into the concentrated elixir of poetry, he offers us a rich tapestry of the colors of life's desires, some muted, others vibrant. He takes us along on his rollercoaster of restlessly twisting and stretching through the unfathomable waves of love and loss - remembered, misremembered, relived, reconstructed. A timely comfort as we collectively acknowledge loss.
– **Sharon Lowen,** major international performing artist, columnist, writer and art historian

Poetry of lost relations and savage longing.
– **Aleyda Rojas**, *Poet, Ecuador*

'Silence is a forest' like Amarendra's poems. Brilliant. Pierces the core. He is an innovative modernist. Profane, yet in the same breath, sacred, brimming with disillusion, yet layered with hope. The man who suffers, and the mind that creates -dissecting and scrutinizing, yet consumed by love and its messy darkness. Amarendra's poems begin with him, and do not end with the reader, but continue beyond, in their relentless, endless sojourn into the forests of infinity, leaving in their wake a lingering wistfulness - restless and thirsty.

– **Sohini Roychowdhury,** Major Bharatnatyam dancer, motivational speaker, women and social issues activist, Founder & Director, Sohinimoksha World Dance & Communications & Sohinimoksha Artes de La India, Madrid

There are very few writers (are there?) who can express so accurately my own feelings better than myself. The masks we wear are torn apart by his images, for they are true, intense, inescapable and therefore liberating. His words throw a light over our darkest shadows and they remind us of a certainty: we cannot live without poetry. An exquisite writer, an impeccable professional, a very dear friend. He is the eternal poet.

– **Mira Tevsic**, eminent musician, journalist, poet and translator, Croatia and Argentina

In Acknowledging Loss *the renowned Indian poet, Amarendra Khatua presents us with a bouquet of poems that he wrote during his stay in Argentina as his country's Ambassador (India).The first thing that strikes you in these poems that flourish in the world, not only as a physical existence, but also as a mirror that reflects the concerns and losses of the self. Nature, memory, love alignment, absence and darkness represent a horizon through which the poet passes towards where he isolates himself in this poetic prophecy. In this, the poet is not far from the Indian cultural and spiritual heritage, which is present in the poem, even if he wrote them in Argentina. Between Indian and Argentina, the poet forms a wonderful poetic imagination provided with images, revelations, metaphors and expressions from various cultural and poetic references, but they are reconciled in the poems in a harmonic and wonderful way.*

– **Mohamed Ahmed Bennis,** Moroccan poet, translator and critic

Poems in this collection, invigoratingly inspiring, presents human nature in disorder with deft precision and beauty and raises a banner of optimism to confront desolation of loss. Love, dreams, desire and waiting – are the paths to our journey into truth and meaning of life. Like a guide with life's experience, the poet presents in his poems the emptiness and the feeling of loss of any contemporary man and his journey into self discovery, through love and lifelessness

– **Stella Maris Ponce,** poet, jazz and tango singer, author of *The Rituals Of The Night* and *The Voice*

Reflection of cosmic and regional experiences is conspicuous in Khatua's poetry. Every word in his poems beads on a contemplative thread. With both asynchronous and contemporary themes, the poet seems estimating and acknowledging the loss that he himself and the world incurred. Poetic devices run through every line as spontaneous as a fountain. The uses of apt imagery and diction transport the readers to some metaphysical world as if they were hobnobbing with speaking pictures. Reading of his poems gives a feeling of waking and open-eyed meditation.

– **Vivekanand Jha,** Air Force Veteran, Indian English Poet, Translator and Editor

Poems in this book meanders through light and darkness. There is a sense of loss as one goes through the book yet there is also an overwhelmingly bright hue which brings back the love for life. Outstanding imagery in every poem this book will inspire readers to practice calm and solitude in the midst of mayhem.

– **Prabal Kumar Basu,** Indian poet

Mincing no words on depths of words, silence, loss, loneliness, acceptance of unfulfilled dreams, imperfect life, social inequalities, yet rays of hopes are visible in the poems for the antagonist to cling on to live, to come back home to face the dark, shadows, or brokenness with equanimity and willingness to search till eternity. Choice of words is impeccable and their impact is great.

–**Mohan Chutani,** Indian Poet

Nirala Series

ACKNOWLEDGING LOSS

Amarendra Khatua is a distinguished Indian poet and Senior Diplomat in the Indian Foreign Service. He has served both as the Indian Ambassador to Argentina, and as the Indian Ambassador to Ivory Coast. A widely traveled author and culture critic, Khatua has forty published collections of poetry in English, Odia, Hindi, and other Indian dialects and international languages.

Acknowledging LOSS

Poems

Amarendra Khatua

Nirala

Nirala Publications
4637/20, Third Floor, 310, Hari Sadan,
Ansari Road, Daryaganj,
New Delhi 110 002
www.niralapublications.com
niralabooks@yahoo.co.in

First Edition 2021

ISBN 978-81-951915-2-9

Cover Design : Tarun Saxena/Graphical House

Cover Art: Aparna Caur

Printed at
Chaman Enterprises
New Delhi-110092

Acknowledgment

Grateful acknowledgment is made to the editors of the journals and anthologies in which some of the poems included in this book first appeared, sometimes in slightly different versions.

Contents

Part Two

Going Away

To Tasha,
my granddaughter

Acknowledging LOSS

Part One

Losing an Address

All About Flying

Is not it the rejection of the
Wind from the fluttering wings, a
Directionless bird can manage?
These birds must be knowingly stupid,
Every winter they have to forego
The tunes and sing for lands that succinctly
Describes exile and distances.
Then as soon as the sparkling
Golden spray of the setting sun
Touches their beaks, they drop into
The foliage, the landscape, the waterless
Wadis and seek nothing.

I wish inside the civilization of my two hundred
And seventy bones I were a bird
Of dimensionless flying! I could
Have touched the speckled dreams
Dying before flicker of eyes,
Wasting the silence of morose
Evenings before a destitute moon
Climbed the muddy clouds. But
This will not be possible in a
Life that grants license to stay
Hungry, when hunger is not beyond
The grasps of love and to stay
Bitter, when starting all over
Again is a matter of touching
Dreams even if one is not asleep.

A Stepping Stone

Inside the forest of my lonely bones,
She weeps for my abject weaknesses. She
Cleans my unseen scabless wounds
Polishes my spent and lost words, and
Hangs around my hurt shadow. Is
Not she the only lie taking shape
Of a woman to mirror my remaining
Betrayals? Or this life time?

She must be a stranger. Though hunger
Eternally remains the only season,
Unchanged and mine, she does not
Mind. I do not think I have let her
To be here. Does she know the
Distance between my longing for her
Physical surrender and my unacknowledged
Private pain of permanence fearing to lose her?
Strangely it seems she knows.
Every time I trip inside the abyss of
Unprinted desires, of carnal
Mumpsimus, she is all tender in
Her eyes, surrounds me with untouched
Devotion in my seeking a way back.
Her eyes are the mirage prints of
Love in sunlight and a tear drop.

This body poisons itself in an
Ocean of published debauchery, everyday.
This fountain of bubbling waywardness
Misses her lips and breasts,
She still does not go away even if

My existential commercials on hara-kiri
Desire disguise me. She is the only lie
In the shape of the woman entitled to retrieve
My remaining faith, to own a soul simply
Remade in love as her crafted gift.

Survival

You must have let half a million accepted
Words in tame hunger and a sticky spat
That broke thirsty two hours including a rainy

Night till we became familiar strangers without
Combed voices and patchwork sex. Even today
The regiment of our twosome history matches

Not on any even keel, with maimed memories. My
Remembering the mole on the left side of
Your stomach below your languid ribcage

Could still generate a sign, unknowingly pleasure
Soaked. Shadow line of your painted smile has
Started receding on the avenue of trumped

Desires. Figments of our heavenly togetherness
Hung on the Moorish wall of semi-constructed
Distances unsettle blank spaces that return

Sometimes. You have grown a world full of
Scented trees, I have decided to live in
A desert of defeated silence, for survival.

Prelude

All the catalogued pictures, familiar to
Me from the days of the marigold sunset
And sandy river bed, refuse to

Return to this cannabis indicted
Exile, to this drunken despair with
No meanings, I continue to fumble for

The lost words, seek them in unopened
Eyes, non-readable lips and unheard of
Distances, sometimes they torture the living,

Raise a forest of self – doubt and
Keep all the prefabricated anguish at a
Safe address hidden from the personal moorings

Easily lost. Yet the floodgate of blind
Waiting incessantly tempt. In the hope
That these unmolested timid words could

Open the pores of tired denials, touch the
Sleepless eyelids and start humming the
Most simple songs eluding me for eons.

On Ophidiophobia

Memories slither in suffocating
Silence. They crawl on tentacles of
Boiling pain and bite into the
Pores of familiar hurt. Fangs of
Lonely routine tortures
Imagination, poisons images so dear.

That is probably why I am
Mortally scared of snakes, my
Whole life.

In my dreams they coil and
Hiss, they throttle colours and
Fill my chest in moving
Angst. I wake up to my daily
Rituals, tired and often bitten.

I am awake. My twenty four
Hours remain as usual a
Thematic curse, between asking
Questions to a life time that
Has no direction and seeking
Roads with names yet
Unfamiliar in their zigzag
Proximity to my destiny.

I have not seen a real snake
Since ages. As soon as I close
My eyes, the silence embracing
Me grows deadlier than a real
Snake all the time, nowadays prying
Movements without life.

For Borges

Silence is a forest. Rootless
Words Perch on filtered sunlight
Shadows dance with rhythm of swaying
Distance, dead with caresses.

You are welcome to trek inside,
To bring unknown sounds with your
Alluring footsteps on the fallen leaves.
A message will whisper into the
Thick embracing branches. Forest has
A bewildered heart, no ears. Eons
Will preserve your coming in cloying
Music of unenhanced proximity. You
Have to leave, trees will die, saplings
Will green with enchanted survival, mutinous
In non committal dignity.

Losing intimate words is like small
Unwoven paths there. Life hustles, love
Dies, it always becomes too late for
The birds to reach the Sky and lose
Their way to a sunset, a hungry palate
Of silence colouring the existence, the Sky.

Silence is the wired torsos, unseen
Roots, the shivering leaves, the spreading
Branches, and finally the whole cartography
Of a crowded green canopy. You have to leave
Before it is dark, before you miss the chosen
Direction. In the surreal presence of
Eternal loss, the forest will note life stories,
Emoting unbearable heartbeats, from afar.

On the Way Back

Seal the sachet of broken bones,
Spray the dust. Count few
Unwritten lines, hatching sunshine
Inside the unspoken exile. Time
To return home, it is. The unattended
Garden has charmed the cursed
Weeds, the name plate is missing. The
Meaningfully melancholic birdsong on
The guava tree across the
Windowed vision must flow in
Usual familiarity.

Does the comfortable shoeless
Present hold you back in the
World of experimental assurances?
How did you accumulate this
Tonnage of desire and desperation in
A sojourn of temporary addresses?

Every meaning must have its
Lost definition, each word an echo
Etched in silent atonement. It is
Time to pack your bags, leave
Behind the notes of stale emotions
And unshed tears. You are the
Hushed poet of dead songs
Littered on the path you chose
But never sought, that should be the
Way it must remain.

Go away, before it is dark. Nights
Possess dark fairy tales that promise
Returns of another lifetime, not your own.

The Wall

Each graffiti has a meaning, a
Celebration and distinct mélange of hues. The
Wall is aware. Each crack has a
Story of lost time, of seasons never
To return and of memories of erasure.
That wall knows.

Have you ever seen the tattered
Prints of last season's posters trying
To hug eternity on the wall? Have you
Felt the tarantula roots roping outside
To retrieve life, sucking the cracks in
Rippling green? The wall can not
Control, but its brick-deep acceptance
And falling colours possesses many songs. History
Hisses, eyes miss.

Please do not demolish this wall of
My unsaid words. I am still mute,
Hungry for a voice and yet to open my
Eyes. This wall is the black board of
Civilization I lay claim on, you stay
Away, the wall also be painted in blood, in red,
As and when needed.

Urban Proverbs

We all kill for pleasure, for
Survival and in war. Then
We construct museums,
Memorials and unpayable pages
Of historical ballads.

We are killed for religion, love,
Faith, betrayal, mistakes and crime.
We are killed by guns, law, shame,
Weather, family and diseases.
But the almanac of remembrance
Only lists those who have
Roads, monuments and books
Dedicated to them.

We all will die one day.
Our mortality is known,
Designated and predestined. Yet
Each death has element of
Profound sorrow and distinct
Colour that starts a picture
Connoting pregnancy.

Dead Memories

I acknowledge. It is
Not mine to give,
This speechless donation
Of private dreams. Dreams
Have sudden endings,
They always spout on the
Precipice of daily living, like the
One way passage seeking your
Bodyless presence.

You belong to all the
Ricocheted attraction converted
Into love. The message must remain
Hidden, encrypted in
Unfulfilled desire and
An ageless hurt.

Still I have to sing, these
Songs are my salvaged
Daily wear. I have to paint,
All primitive colours are
Tinted with my amaranthine waiting.
Some lines may touch your heart
And flower into the canvass
Of impure magic.You will be somewhere,
Encasing enchantment.

I confess, it is never in my
Control to not to
Wake up in the middle of the
Night, under a touch

Of unseen aroma and feel
Your absence seized by
Hungry sighs and shrouded by
Dead memories.

A Picture Poem

You do have to weep over the
Dying lotuses. The water level is again
Almost right to sprout new

Dreams. You can see the images of the
Trees, the sky, all the dots to be calculated as
Flying birds and your darkness in

The waveless surface. If you start
Crying, your tears will not have the
Power a torrential raindrop carries.

They will mostly plop arousing self-pity
And disappoint. You must know, all these
Flowers charming the water bed with

Managed memories carry history and
Hurt, all with predetermined prophecy
Those must die and become folklore.

Imagined stories weave satin dreams
And never construct daily rituals for persons
Scared of water in all seasons.

Image of the Word

Never uttered the word
That I always learnt by
Rote to kill for,
Never memorized the word
That stayed absent in my
Soul as a pretext and did
Not flourish.

Never created the word
Even if my salvation begged
My body all the time,
Never banished the word
That created a hovering darkness
Beyond my routine and survival.

Never sustained the word in
Courage and conviction, stolen
And borrowed.
Never pictured the word in
Prayers dying on lips yet
Burdening on immorality.

Now the world has constructed a
Galaxy of its own and I, the
Eternal outsider, am knocking
At the door for such a late
Entry of eternal silence into
Wordlessness.

Unseen

Blind from birth,
I lose my way
Seeking destiny and you.

I must lose always,
Losing is my faith, religion
And diversity. Also a mask.

My losses have their own
Hamlets, houses emanating
Sunrise and promises never to arrive.

These losses only make me as I am.
I remain the sightless eternity,
Moments on fire from the time you create.

Now confessions provide little
To salvage. Losses scavenge inside
Soul, dredge prayers into

Litany of absences. My eyes
Cannot see, but the pulp of imagination
Still looks for you, all the time, blindly.

Getting Nowhere

Darkness halts and whispers. The
Forest possesses dead soul
Rotting with dignityless hunger.

I unpeel aged memories into any
Journey. I have no feet, pendulum
Of existential lethargy can never be

A good time keeper. Then everything
Flees. Your face, my unsaid words,
Our naked bodies in shadows –

Everything flees. Horny dew drops
Cover the gaping eyes, rare petals blink in
Mourning. Not that I cannot bleed

Into echoes, in tears hidden for
Molten love, morbid hopes! I have to
Bake happiness, leave the disturbed

Spaces, seek a distance that does not
Bite, away from snarling scorching
Dreams. It is the time to undertake

A tryst. Undone love, morose physical
Falls under love pretext. Next turn
Is my last ditch pause, must start from here.

For Waiting

Broken wings emit
Fallen songs. Wind whimpers
Under runaway clouds and
Colourless buds weigh down
Shivering branches.

Dreams enchant the flight
Addressless destination
Hovers around love's season.
Blind eyes can see the face,
Your body and togetherness as
A stitched picture forever.

Despite golden light covering
The patches of unfulfilled promises,
The day will be eaten up. Corroded
Shadows will embrace waiting.
Poor fragile wings will be touched
By your departure, séance of loss.

Compose all your songs now in
Eerie expectation. Do not give them
Any prescribed tune. Let them rush
Into blind wind, rustle the broken
Wings. They say love hides miracles
And flying may be recouped through your
Mute serenades.

Counting Loss

I know I will fail. My feet will
Be unable to carry the tonnage
Fossilized by a wasted past. Everyone
Will mark the tottering steps
Missing curated threshold, part decorated
In enchantment, rest in delicate question marks.

Failure is contaminated civics. I always
Fall in love, lose my moorings, my manhood and
A civilised sense in containing my sorrows.
I am perpetually scared of death, snake bites,
Seismic shifts and fear of returning to the
City where heart asks simple questions
And body will seek sinful offerings.

I have not been schooled by immortal
Memories. I bought the days when
A wound blessed me accepting
Love as profuse bleeding, but I remember being
Attended by faithlessness knowingly.

I am destined to lose you in all
The frames edited by antipathy
Nurtured inside loss. Love will prevail, but
Never in my knowing that we are
Just together for now only and never after.

Salvaging self

I am lost perpetually in the
Stock market of borrowed dreams. I sell
Wanton waiting as shares and all I
Can afford to buy are promises to myself only.
This life provides many pictures vivid
With intimate failures. Fail, I must, and
The serpentine journey into accumulating
Losses and counting wounds continue.

Aware of all the colours bestowed during
Nine months inside mother's womb; prepared
For the fiery battle which will slay demons
And desire, destiny and resolutions; weather
Beaten in seeking love which bites and maims,
Togetherness which matures into nothingness – I
Am all you can see, can not feel, can touch
But can not saturate in mortal enchantment.

Let me be. If the next call outside the
Frontiers of waiting is yours, I can not be
Unprepared in the field of abandoned
Melancholia. Love is grace when fulfils, love
Curses me otherwise in the conjugation of
My betrayed understanding and her prescribed
Departure, everytime. Let me float in the dreams'
Despair, awakening may hold salvation, dearly wanted.

Going On

I can not afford to
Leave any foot prints
Behind. Destiny carries its
Own manicured curses
And repeals history sans
Love and in revenge, foregoing
All my acknowledgements.

Even if I am eternally
Scarred, I have to draw
My personal losses in acute
Maps. The atlas of hungry
Yesterdays will always
Torture my desire and dreams
Fermenting a future
Riding your unrequited promises
Will not let me die and just
Go away
From the assembly of your
Unhinged attractions.

Dateless dying is not my
Choice. My life is not
Controlled by cozy time lines
Decimated by self. You have
To decide now
If the empty landscape
Littered with my dedicated
Melancholia
Can bring you back and
Make me walk again
Towards you
In love without using feet.

A Lost Letter

I believe it carried adequate
Postage stamps with a correct
Address and a hesitant note.

The words themselves did not matter
Much, emphasized relevance when
Not required, yet borrowed wantonly from love.

How could presumed love carry a
Letter devoid of a personal sky
Silencing cooing pigeons to its destination? The post

Man must have guessed the lightness
Of the practiced songs burrowing in
Hunger yet expressing nothing to

Breed acceptance. How many years back
The letter missed its unpaved direction
And now started haunting memories in
Bracketed itches in silence, life size!

Picturing Loss

The adoral plant must grow
Into a shrub of reconciled words.
Few chattering birds must adorn
The shivering branches coining rare
Songs for lost lessons.
I will hum myself into an arriving
Journey again. The day will darken
Under frivolous moon caressing
Broken clouds. My songs will reach all
Of you in borrowed attires
Stitched by love and departure.

Always beginning has its eerie
Shadows. Life forgives, love abandons.
A shard of faith cuts into
Palpitating memories and memory bleeds.
Someone should have taught
The days to reincarnate into throbbing
Silence, nine months of tunes
Etched in nubile silence.

Retreat

Broken words
Pave silently
The path I used for
Immortality and you
Left feeling unwanted.

Now the path is all dusty,
Bed of fallen leaves
And weave meaninglessness
Into banal distances.
I have died a thousand times
Bereft of personal milestones,
You wait across there
Surrounded by my personal sunset.

We could have sat down
On the grass before we trod
Over dreams and walked away from hope.
Same words would have coiled
Into achievable hunger, related belongingness.
Now the path does not capture
Any song we shared. I have lost
My way outside dead seasons, you
Pluck flowers without knowing loss
Of my enchanted homecoming.

Time for Things

Must be early evening hours, not yet
Dark. Lazy pictures fall from the
Tired trees, broken leaves of
Homecoming. A lonely dragonfly
Flicks away distance atop moving
Shadows. Hunger waits for moonlight
To dazzle the pearl interior of a
Dew drop. Before liquid darkness
Entered my world, an asthma attack of
Primordial silence seeks all our sorrows.
Sky is the length, vacant stars and
Cracked speechless waiting in changing
Colours.

Darkness is the island of heavenly
Indifference. Across the map floats
Images catered by dormant dreams,
Lakes of stupefied promises. This
Early, no promise of any dusk could
Surround the empty Belly of the
Unseen night with hushed haloes,
Starry meanings, aroma-laden sigh
Of fleeting Clouds. Darkness is all
There to living, pale coma for
Counting sins and seeking love.

It is not yet dark, waylaid songs
Are yet to return to the table of
Unkempt routine. Love has to curl
Next to the unmade buds of unnamed
Flowers. Sleep may reincarnate into

Any understanding beyond single
Death, never to have love and preserved
Dreams of molten imagination. All have
To be dedicated plainly in the name
Of life, it is not yet dark, moon must
Appear first.

In Another Country

In my country
You are welcome to borrow
The Nuance of many
Failed history. But you
Must cry when the folded
Corners of the map
Bleed in borrowed hopes.
Hopes die here amid
Throbs of razed dreams,
We butcher them.

Did not we erect the statues
That breathed life and decorated
Our celebrations with messages
Of eternal prosperity? In my
Land, fossilized avatars
Sing for duty and preach
Progress. And many villages
Die and a city slum
Awakens to the principles
Of begging bowls. Charity never
Begins

I am only a foot soldier. I
Salute the sunrise, the cloud
Of dust that brings tears to
My eyes when the flag flutters
And the anthem seeps into my
Uneducated soul. I know, I
Must kill when this spread
Of millennia appears clothless
Today and when the tomorrow
Is hidden by calculated
Promises sucking blood
And faith.

Losing Words

Silence ululates
Inside
A dead forest of
Wriggling words.
These poor words
Bloated on
Savagery of
Human innocence
Once ruled
Many hearts and
Created miracles.

Now silence cannot
Digest them in
Pure rejection nor
Can disgorge
With passionate
Abandon. Unheard
Noises voice rumours
And surreal dreams
Crowd in.

I always celebrate
Silence
Because I lost all
My words
Looking for music
Planting eternity.
Each drop of synthetic
Fulfillment
Chartered lonesome fall

From the precipice of
Love and died in
Famine of primeval
Muteness, anchoring my
Soul.

Now my world
Retains its stupefied
Memories. Silence
Craves soiled images of
My desire
And post songs of
Waiting reverberating
In hopelessness

My Country

Every morning
When the sun rises
Like a baked sunflower
Over a thatched roof tilted
In any nameless countryside,
Do you see the movements
That ideate inside empty stomachs
With buds of cultured hopes?
A naked chest of a child
Burning with dreams for
Bread and words?
A women praying for her
Unseen hero and endangered chastity?
Many leaders of half baked words
Sprouting fluid sentences
And well meaning betrayal?

Where are our presence, the
Doubting civilization of
Middle class virtues and
Achievements, creating a movement
Of hopes and happenings?
It is our doing, the
Mahabaharat of unmade destiny
Will surely curse us with the
Beauty of living surrounded
By the dirt of distress. We
Tell the truth with closed
Eyes and inside the prison of
Sacrificeless individualism.

The map has to bleed in front of
Our impotence. We are the
Sons and forefathers of our
Tomorrow, poor country, we are
Entrenched duly in our takings
From the bloodied soil.

Losing an Address

Darkness displays all the word, broad avenues of our soul,
No pavements of instant pleasure. You seek the unknown
Stars and a blatant moon, not of this Night's making. You suffer.

Have you ever purchased a small plot of
Impure happiness when heart cries?
Do you acknowledge the unheard rhythm
that batters your existence, yet practices
Skosh inheritance of waiting
Before you seek meaning?

Your own familiar night has all these
Wonderful diversions and your
Dreams in its furious claws. You always
Beg for redemption from emptied
Relationships all the time

Darkness has a spell, you know.
You walk alone and always return
To the cubicle of strangled memories.
Memory possesses a city and you
Have lost your pincode of love
And her identity, stop complaining now.

Stalemate

Can not string a touch of
Intense Desire here, this is the
Framed anguish of moonlit nights
And a hovering cloud, aloof and hungry.

I pass my time here in the backyard of
Designed routine. My shadows wither
And all the doorways carry the same
Messages painted by hollering darkness. ButI
Cannot leave before the season of dead
Flowers bedeck this body
With promiselessness.

You have to know. Somewhere inside the
Empty circle of impure heartbeats
A waiting catches Fire. You never
See how it rains for countless days
And one night before a limp rainbow
Climbs on my soul and sends me back
To my room filled with negatives
Of loss, never to be developed in this life.

For Tasha

My fingers grow feathers,
Your smile makes them flutter.
Birds of affection in
Multitude crowd my daily living.
You become the Sky
With a gaping toothless mouth and noisy Eyes.

I always knew,
My mortality had a
Profile in ages, numbers and in
Accumulation of necessary
Uselessness imposed by destiny.
You are the golden frame around
My annotated living and I
Become immortal before dying.

See, this is the string which floats
In the year and with me pushing it.
See the end of the string has
My love seized in your tiny fingers and edging
Towards your curious mouth. See, these are the
Trees in winters, cleaning the
Vista outside the window with
Our togetherness and barking
Under light jumping from your eyes.

My granddaughter, I throw
Open the maps I had drawn in
Grandeur of conquering life,
You don't have to accept
Anything, but be there
And see how I struggle to live
For another eternity, everyday.

Kites

Atticful Disneyland of morose memories can
Have similar sense of accounting footfalls
Only you can recognise, mark and pass the afternoon
Bookmarking shadows.

A chalk white moon will struggle inside the
Branches of fluffy clouds tell you will shiver with
The familiar darkness descending inside your

Expectant bones in hungry tides, of things lost,
Relationships distorted and till you are returned unfulfilled
To the shores of wrong passages, life passing by.

The mutant inventory must be maintained in the haze of pallid
Stories. Nothing will be left whole to dig inside
The buried autobiography and discover new baby
Steps to start anew. Broken desires tend
To hang like bats in Sleepless continuity yet
Nudge you to imprisoned departures never forgotten.

The picture is all about dead kites, afloat
Once in an indefinable abandon, now preserved
For the sense of the wild wind serrating
The mind, their hearts now cannot race nor soar, they
Are floating absences piled in colours, shapes,
Sizes and multilated, all dead kites and all
Preserved, never to fly again.

Invitation

Moonlight of hazel reflections has wasted
My body, bewitched stars have emblemed my
Eyes with shadowy desire in twinkling glaze.

Will you come? Before the spent aroma of
Unknown flowers rush out of the ajar
Window of this being, unspent sleep touching the

Skin, raw and remaining! Will you come?
The lingering Waves of hunger will be caressing the
Unmade murals of etched waiting, an

Universe of seeking, palpitating in shimmering
Rain. Séance time, the raps are crossing the
Threshold of tempted bones. It is the time

For Tides of your acceptance touching my
Unidentified allure. In knee-deep invitation
A night prospers, sharpened and slithering,

Will you come?

Notebook lines for my great grandfather

Growing old, he drawled, is like
An epidemic which has never been
Cured, but very few can endure a
Garlic breath mortality still wanting
To grow desire in darkness and
Preen in shamelessness.

Hold your liquour, he pronounced, till
Your own reflection becomes vapour,
Prompts a hazy sky and then
Pure deathless dreams. Hold your
Horses till your own personal
Dreams are ready to surrender in
The name of love and friendship
And detonate into pure absences
When waiting touches you and
Unbecomes.

My great grandfather was a
Born Sharman, always carried a
Small tote bag of lust, bit of
Soothing drugs and a bottle of colourless
Hooch. Hung on my fragile back,
Unprotected, is the bonsai of
His loans in love, interpreted in many
Years of decorated space,
Singularly polluted by self-doubt,
Framed in grainy imagination.
Old age, he had added is like
A star you can see in the evening,
Tomorrow it will die in a vacant
Sky, in the dump of stardust heap
Seeking unwritten obituaries.

Part Two

Going Away

Tongo Notes

i

On the toe, flashes the
Bent knee upward reverse
And whips between your
Dancing steps. Hold my
Upturned face, see the
Lips shiver.

Before I jump into your
Folded embrace, let the
Music flood my mobile body
Into a labyrinth of
Dance eternity.

ii

Melancholy washing the
Colours, restlessness in the
Piano cry. Feel the lightening
Steps caressing the earth
And your invitation amid the
Dance lust, music lust.

Watch your hands around my
Gyrating waist, watch your bending lips
And let the tango begin before
We are into us and we are lost.

iii

You touch my cheek and hold
My face in your palms, my
Supple fresh flowers into
Numerous branches of attended
Hunger in circling steps.

I surrender a body that
Axels into monuments of
Forbidden expression,
Shining from the assembled
Shadows, we create
On stage.

iv

Put your hand softly on
My shoulder
Till my body bends in a
Divine stoop seeking
Your lips.

And let the halo encircle
Our dance till a forest
Of movements grow knee -high
In cloying symphony of
Dancing music, dancing life.

A Krsna Poem

i

Every finger will lift mountains,
Each kiss will produce music that will
Enchant and detonate a flute.

Every departure will destroy hamlets,
Cities and footsteps. Each word will
Speak in symbols carrying only

Purity of life, outside death will reign.
Each pore will throb with energy where gods will
Live with desire and destruction, every moment

Will have its truth, obtainable justice and curses
Afloat from honour and shame, dignity and
Defeat. Before pathos will become a text or a

Hymn to the history of empires and belongings,
He must leave, with or without friends, with
No lover, death hovering atop kingdoms built

Over eons. Then he will pause to virtually
Test is own self and ask questions which
Nobody could answer. Thus prayers will

Become designed songs with many interpretations.
Each song will seek him in formless
Love, begging understanding.

ii

Memories will not landfill the dread, hunger
Will rule.The women will have to nourish
From their own desire, bodily heat will become

Litanies that can never be sung. Theblue
Bones will jump atop a fuming serpent
And dance amid flowering trees and a herd of
Bare chested women defying a overflowing
River. Theman boy will anoint families in
Ecstasy yet will weave a destiny to

Shipwreck hamlets, curse dynasties and
Choreograph violence into holy wars everywhere
The dead will pile up in nameless

Numbers, widows will lose identities and
Hundred children, somewhere more desire
Will sprout bloody red flowers, without

Aroma. He will not wait for the beggar
Friend nor for cruel kings nor for a
Beloved aging into molten bones and waiting

This story will have its own lyric never to
Be assembled into human forms, yet
All his songs will arouse strange emotions elbowing faith.

Songs Foretold

(i)

This is the body of a
Small man,
A mind of dense jealousy.
I preach what I cannot hear
And dance with the sounds
Of broken promises.

Yet everytime the profane
Word pierces my heart,
Here I return again and again
With touches, polishing this
Sepia world, with the
Aroma of eternity, of your love.

(ii)

This is why I open up
But never in love
What I surrender is tagged
As my destiny.
But always my feminine shelf
Breaks into
Destinationless entities of
Nothingness.

Then you ask for love
Without my
Acknowledgement.

(iii)

Songs do answer
But life has no songs.
When this life has so little meaning
Without your prompting presence

Now that you are there
I invite all the songs to appear
They hide
With the malice of your acceptance

And appears a gap with
The haiku of not knowing what I wanted.
(iv)

Never I could capsule the sentiments
And your time just missed my way

But the burden of your recognition
In love, giving and tuning the
Stony beats of my heart
Into something that the
Faith only can cherish

Make me return from the defeat,
From the rejection and even from death

And to wish
That same broken lips will sing,
The broken body will retrieve
The unmade songs of love.

Negation

Never so simple. How could
A nine month old blind
Embryonic journey
Muster so much blues for a
Whole battling lifetime, yet
Nonchalantly sing for love, never redeemable!

Living is practiced begging, so
Well rehearsed. A prayer for mental
Peace, a relationship to awaken
The decimated hungry animal
Curled inside the ribs, a home
To store dreams and confront
Dead memories and the life for
Everyone to see and secrets of
Longing and waiting for yourself.

The day the umbilical cord is
Detached from the assurance
Of the Mother's body, the war
Rages. Rote of destiny roars
Inside the cranium. Heartbeats
Roll in Wonder and awe, appointed
By shadowy banalities. The mirror
Empties out millions of reflections,
Never one exacting the desire
Seeping your aorta

Also it is not easy to stand
In the public square and beg
For love and happiness. Lifestyle
Dissuades, love abstains.

Rehearsing Loss

Rejection open up its
Empty palm. Each line,
Depicting vagaries of stolen
Stories, points out to retreating
Steps, imagined moments and spent
Waiting. Then the open palm of
Swollen expectation never
Closes, never.

It was always told, the
Unheard prayers have the
Power to cleanse, to mend the
Darkness inside the soul and
To rescue and prepare for the difficult
Journey again. Where are the
Words that picture a prayer
Confronting the vast abyss of
Rejection, life size?

Now the prolonged routine will
Have its prescribed chores. Life
Will open windows, close many
Doors, stoop to pick up dead
Petals and borrow smiles. A
Small scar will transgress the
Protective spheres around the
Heart and mirror the sadness,
Almost forgotten knowingly.

Emoting Loss

Silence was coiling
Like the aroma of unknown
Flowers inside your eyes.
Painted silvery clouds
Hung under a chalk white
Erotic moon. You spoke in
The silkiest voice of the
Dark inviting night. Your words
Gargled in the throbs of
Asking for love and
Flanked my waiting moments
In a cloying stupor, of some
Half-made dreams and rest in
Pure parched skin hunger

And I retreated.
Emotion had no limbs, no pretext,
Yet my bones receded in sighs.
The seeking palm remained unopened
For promises that our flesh
Could have weaved. My eyes
Turned away on their own
Betrayal of physical essence, while
You waited.

Now neither can I retrieve my
Wanton footsteps into the
Garden of your unadorned invitation,
Nor can you wait with preserved
Eternity for recognition of my
Love simply untrespassed
In the Seasons of my fall.

Love Hurts

Leaving behind the portion of impersonal
Neglect will not qualify. Love has its own
Sanctuary of preserved memories. This stadium of

Desperate abandon processes dead pictures
Of our purest lust, our bodily allure. We carry
Chiselled hunger inside our unpolished bones

Till we prey upon love and love hurts us in
Bountiful torture. Now any debate over our
Deserting relationship, the art of trite coupling

And a life self spending dreams is not
Of your making, our control. You have signed off
In the name of lost love before you mended your

Own hunger. Now darkness without personal
Intimacy spreads restlessness and you need only love.
And love really hurts, mutilating all seasons.

Departing

Exile is my foster home.
As my desire do not have
Their own fulfilling wings, I
Always have to go away
From the city of your
Rare invitation.

But tell me, can you wipe
Away this footsteps of the
Dazzling falls that
Memory recreates?
Remember, you called my name, a
Strange tree with aborted foliage
Flowered off season
And I retraced your body
In branches of hunger, probably
With twigs of love.

Your breast still bear the marks
Of my banishment
In your giving. Your thighs
Easel my throbs of
Enchanted manhood in our
Acceptance. Yet I have
To leave in not
Belonging to your awakening
Against my ballistic pretense
To possess you.

This is my eternal profile of
Departure also of my lust.
Love is the shadow
Eclipsed by our pact where
You will always seek me
And I would have left eons back.

Your Poetry

The chopping blade of mutant words
Processes distinct hunger for our
Pet failures. Poetry will certainly ask for a
Sacrifice, you know, when you will be
Constructing an artificial bomb shelter to protect
Yourself from any emotional raid. Itwill
Claim your weaving faith when
You will be trying to hide all that
You believe in love yet pawned
In personal rejection.

Nobody paves the unseen path for you
In musical certainty. You walk
Under the beguiling lights of shadowy
Stars. You borrow from heart, from
Pulsating veins, you save from the
Scenes without sensory affiliation.
Poetry covered in warmth, in
Serene pictures of defined moments
And your surrender, just strolls by.

Do you know that same
Curved knife lines of eternal
Silence will scrap your bones
For seasonal songs, when songs belong
To echoes of personally dead moments?
You also never learnt that poetry
Could inspire dark empire
Inside your heart, your crafting
Silo, absolutely distinct from what
You could deliver in your sincerest

Offering in creative afterlife.

Poetry does not get used to taking prisoners
Of War. It just kills in absence and
It ruminates all kind of mental distances in
Abhorrent madness. You have to
Prepare to live for poetrylessness in
Your own way.

Playing Field

You hide inside a
Photo frame of intimate
Shadows, I throw colours
Outside.

The margin of daily living is
Immensely narrow. Blades of
Melancholia cuts into insecure
Dreams. You immediately look
For me, I miss to be there, inside
The threshold of your pet anxieties.

Our story will always leave a number
Of empty pages in our togetherness.
You acknowledge, I feign attachment.
I return, you are now bound by dear
Silence, etched by waiting.

Just knowing that your library of
Feminine discovery
Has a stack of translated feelings
Dedicated to my desires
Is enough for me to go on
Seeking you. You go, the world has
Floated on a cloud of
Cruel thorns. Let me pluck the
Flowers of adequate love, one
Day I will fulfil you.

Living Loss

Sometimes the loss appears
Next to your life-size routine. You
Pretend as if in your mental list
Anything that does not have dimension
To elate never existed. The irritating
Pause struggles inside your chest. You
Sigh, then mundane question marks
Take over.

Isthis the hide and seek mind plays
With living? Half merged pictures of
Happiness and possession superimposed
Over passing time! The loss always
Has its intensity, a dark sense
Stuttering and stuck on the anvil of
Angular existence. You bet on the
Reasons clamouring for you to go
On with everything and nothing. Yet the
Feeding borrows a hollow nest
Inside your uneven days, hungry
Nights.

Even you can print the calligraphy of
Loss before finding love again, redefining
The new spaces you are yet to belong.
But loss is poetry that haunts, tunes
That curl inside your harping
Bones. You sleep in the bed of essential
Life, loss turns side next to you
Every night, this lifetime.

Rereading Loss

Too dark to see your face,
My stretched hand touches
Absence.
Are you there? Riding the sound
Wave of mysterious meaning
And my grateful sighs?

I Wish I knew. Always the
Poetics of bodily hunger
Taught me the music of Loss. And
Never a single heartbeat
Practiced on its own
Spending a day without sunshine
Of your feel, a single night without
The rainfall of darkest petals
From your body.

Now I am as blind as the
Horoscope of a lost Love. I am
The voiceless search of my
Waitings, seeking incarnation into
Your return. So silent
To ache with your surrender,
My days beg to my destiny, you
Must see, the fall of eternity.

You will not return I know.
I know I will borrow pleasure
And buy definitions in my
Lifetime. You will remain in the
Dark, in my seeking, in my haunted
Existence and I will manage
Without love, yet in love
Somehow.

Life Time

These spent words
Will not be able to
Sing for love anymore
Nor can they rehearse
Memories of colours
Drowning inside heartbeats.

These words are
Like a supine dead
Porcupine crucified
In its own quills, lay
Coiled into immobile
Indifference, beyond resurrection.

Why would anyone relate
To disposable dead words? Are not
Their scrapping one's bones
Dream dry enough? Are not
Their cursed murmurs inside
Sleepless time killing too loud?
They are, yet why do they persist like
Unseen teardrops, pictureless poems!

The all have to reside in the
Garden of uneven seasons. A
Patch will carry the plaster of
Dead words and others will
Attempt new buds of deliberate
Salvaging work in life. These dead
Words will linger on, time will
Pass, life will crash and one day
An eerie silence will try to
Resurrect the same lifeless words in
Our relationless fiction.

Confession of a Difficult Man

She stumbles and falls,
I hear. Not a single day
Passes by when I do not
Whore my blind eyes and
Stay hidden.

I am not blind by birth.
My wingless dreams
Populate my corrupt world.
She mumbles and prays,
I curse. The days grow
Into habituated cruelty,
We just exchange symbols.

We are not other people. We
Build a house and christen the
Doormats into a home. We
Craft nine months into a
Beautiful future, a child
Is named. Then the apnea
Of daily passage
Unburdens a whole picture
Of insincerity. She knows,
I wish I knew!

Where are the groping hands
In stemful of happiness?
She never blames, I store
My binges and lust under
My borrowed shadows. Now I
Wear her pain as my
Accomplishment and she continues
With life as if nothing
Has happened, in my admission
Of a pretense that I forgive no more.

Infidelity

You said, you are a married man and
Opened your lips to kiss me. I probably
Did not utter a thing. Then kissed you at

That moment, an absent face tore like a
Bunch of origami roses of crisp handmade
Paper, before we kissed again. The arena of

Hungry shadows dance around us in open
Carousal. Did I acknowledge the rippling face
Of falling sparkles! The contours of many

Preserved moments that I lost for counting
The beads of cloying hunger? Now the pages of
Family album miss few favourite photographs

Where my eyes are aglow with seeking
Prescribed identities and my days are
Not replete with broken punctured reflections

Of mine haloed by falsetto desires.

Dear Father

With a surrogate package of irritating dualities,
Dear father, am I turning into another you, your

DNA-soaked dialects grafted as a pretender of
Immense beginnings and a personal intolerance?

I wish I delved into the secrets of all our familial
Distances, the penury of the art that loses so much

In tame biographies. Then it is so difficult to begin
All over inside a buzzing silence, wordlessness clinging

Into the nights of exile, yet definitely familiar
To oneself, my sins are all sold away in the

Pawnshop of judgmental reflections. Yet I cringe
As soon as your shadow, hello father, crosses the

Threshold of controlled pauses before trying to define this
Life, any whichway I fail to fathom.

To Begin Anew

A new home
Has a fragile foundation
Made of dreams. You
Must seek your address
Anyway, familiar
Mantle places to position
Your family photographs
And to wait for messages
From a past
Coloured in imagination
Exiled but always hungry
To keep you awake in
Vivid refugee crayons.

The broken path left behind
Inside maps swollen in dust,
Poverty, genocide and mutated
Tree trunks, the hazy
Horizon mispronouncing departures
With middle class hollywood prints
And bodies, dead, missing, tired,
Hungry, molested and seeking, always
Reaching strange shores somehow.

Human dreams are of many
Distinct religions, no one can
Name it with a god's face or inside
A familiar space. The dread
Bustling inside heart in search
Of practiced illusions
In many pristine forms present

Temples, churches, mosques,
Cities, countries and unions
But no defined cultural pores, moral
Belongings.

Now all pictures are
Dedicated to your
Looking for a home, a
Temporary address for now.
The landscape is
Dotted with a dead baby
In flowery dress floating
In blue waters, a pair of
Hungry eyes of a young man
Scorching a vacant sky, a
Svelte body of a wandering
Women ravaged inside a
Rudderless boat and curious
And waiting eyes of ours.

It is an art house of lost
Memories where your hopes
Struggle for new hopes,
New beginnings.

Accepting Loss

You promised me
A life of eternity
Perfected in
Unusual betrayal,
Filled with existential
False ceiling
And never fully belonging
To me
Neither controlled by me.

Then you also prescribed to
This disfigured creature
Battling its own
Nightmares, fallen choices
And unwanted demons.
Sowing acres of
Melancholic
Songs in fields of daily
Living to bath
In the Ganges of
Waiting and self discovery
And metamorphosed
Into your own shadow,
Your own image yet in
Mortal frame of
Beautiful renewal, still
Without salvation.

Every time a plunderer
Discovered a sacred story
Teller, I appeared

As the pages unfulfilled
For you to edit.
Whenever history
Abandoned a city, a God
Died in the forest and
Tears of naked women ran
Parallel to a river drowning
The city, I had to be
Appeared as any reincarnated
Picture, you had to colour.

I accepted the curse
And chanted in silence for
The world
Impregnated by desolate
Foraging of all corrupt
Space. I also awaited for your
Donation from this dark
Arenaof suffered address,
Every drop of water pearl
Washing away
My sins and my
Prayers blooming into a
Flowering lotus supplementing
Light and awakening to this life,
Here.

For Vidyapati - 1

I used all my captive words
And create a personal Silence. I hate all kind of
Music that uses me to hum your
Absence and make me cry.

Believe me, all my confessions on the pew of
Naked routine seek a simple prayer,
Haloed by your love. They are not
Donated by your recognition, they only
Echo my life chosen by acute desires
Of unreciprocated intensity colouring our lost moments.

Now, I do not value my words
So much. Words possess. Youexist
As the interpretation of my borrowed
Karma betraying my hunger
Of soul seizing my lifetime. These
Words also keep me awake
Without the pet dream of my pretended
Rebirth into your love, your love being the
Séance of footsteps only I can remember.

For Vidyapati - II

Sometimes we forget to return
The bids that polished our
Rough diamond existence into love
And exhilaration. The borrowed pleasures
Lives in darkness like scattered
Whimpers of unseen bats in the attic.
Of saturated flesh and enflamed hunger.
We go on constructing tame figures of
Routine outside our reach. The hazy
IOUS of forgiven relationships still remain
Intact ulcered in unkempt memories.

One day a day will envelop
The whole scaffold of our rare dreams,
A touch will embrace the twinkle
Of the sweet pain below the heartbeats. Will
We be able to recall the deep
Nuances of our nonchalant belonging to
The fall, once? Will our eyes be able to retrieve the
Broken images that embalm
Our dead waiting into few moments of
Beautifully crafted songs?

We always forget. Whenever
Return the unopened borrowings
In love and in betrayal.
We are always destined to
Use the crutches, the ones
Our heart throws back to us
Into the begging bowl of our preserved memories.

Positioning Loss

The way I place my tatami
Next to the painted wall is
My unique style. All my
Knives and swords have anger
Etched on their blades. Now
Killing myself could be only a
Banal ritual, hara-kiri must be
Rehearsed neatly by myself so
As to allow you to keep the
Order and wipe your wall clean
Of unwanted blood and not to
Count empty stands missing
Tongues of honed hostilities.

Where did I learn shadowing my
Hunger for your betrayal into
Inviting death? Stress is mostly
Evading small escapes outside
Innocence. Very few are really innocent.
Life burgles inside the house of love
And coherence. Now nobody justifies
Why a killing must ensure my salvation
From your world where love still remains
Alphabetless and death constructs artforms.

Rerun

Somehow we have to discard the moments
That do not border on our hedonistic
Hunger for love and identity. We also have

To decide on the remaining baggage in
Prescribed memories that we can carry with
Us pretending ownership. Can we then

Sit down under a sepia sky and keep
Our fingers interlaced in an indefinable tenderness?
As if we had kept on waiting for sustaining this

Love in the name of many untold sufferings painted
Without our knowledge, yet embryonic in our
Making them. We always have to die in love yet love must

Come before death, gala dinners, destiny foretold
And divine warning. We carry on and practice
The ancient art where no one has to measure

Exact depth of love and memories must lapse
On their own like timid tides never to return to
The womb of a fugitive ocean.

Empty Space

Missing people, places and
Occasionally things is
Like religions.

Religion always preaches such
Beautiful isolation, yet all the resplendent
Prophets and gods fight wars, conspire
To kill, steal from family and elope
With strangers. I am a mere mortal,
Seeking glamour in silence and
Ignoring all full stops resembling death.
I miss all fallen seconds, every
Distanced face all the time in unspent pain.

Missing wounds me always, not
Mortally though. Missing also plants
An orchard of hurt inside my heart,
Never with a tree that can be identified for
Growing fruits for eternity.
Nowadays I start my routine
Crossing off days that never end
And omitting nights that prowls in
Sleeplessness. My waiting begins to
Fester my enchantment soaked in absences.

Intimacy of Loss

I eviscerate all the broken shadows
From your pain and suffering. I
Wear All your losses like throbbing
Pendants welding starlight with deeper
Meaning. I cannot be a prophet at all, I
Am the last burning step before
Darkness hobbles into history never
To be read again.

Your waiting break all rhythms of my
Primeval awakening. I lose love in
Distance, faith in absence, relationships
In seeking and all substance in hunger.
Then my shoulders are ready to carry
All your monumental sorrows. My feet
Are willing to struggle and inch towards
An address you may seek, but will not keep
Forever.

I am merely the shadow master baked
By all your shadows, hunting dreams painted
In ebony tears raining through eons
Of personal pain, incessantly.

Going Away

You please continue to watch rain,
Raindrops carry music and magic.
Let broken rainbow lines shadow
My vision, I am inside a doorless
Windowless waiting, I cannot borrow
Your love and my destiny.

You may have a garden of your own,
A readymade definition which
May not bring a giggle but can
Be used to paint your smiling
Lips. You have dancing steps to
Seek love, yet remain happily
On a lifesize bed of acute
Distance.

I am so far away, away from
The orphaned dreams loaned by
Your recognition. You continue
To touch the raindrops on your
Fingertips, I still walk away,
Wet and showered by the whispering
Shadows.

All our exchanges flout their
Own seasons, own cycles of silent
Films. Our love probably lives
Inside the emergency ward of
Broken memories under this halting
Melancholic raindrops. You
Go on watching the rain, I can
Not break a hole inside this
Loveless prison to see the lightning,
Kissing the raindrops in shimmering hope.

From The Beginning

We all kill for pleasure,
For survival and in War.
We construct mausoleums,
Memorials and unplayable pages
Of historical ballads.

We are killed for religion, love,
Faith, betrayal, mistakes and crime.
We are killed by Guns, law, shame,
Weather, family and disease.
But the almanac of remembrance
Only lists those who have
Roads, monuments and books
Dedicated to them.

We all will die one day.
Our mortality is known,
Designed and predestined. Yet
Each death has elements of
Profound sorrow and distinct
Colour that starts a picture
Connoting pregnancy.

Miscalculating Loss

Your vision has much depth,
Calculable span, reason to
Recognise, acknowledge and
Adequate madness to respond.
But your heart has linked space,
Often emotionally auctioned.

Now tell me, how can I just
Pluck a flower, decide on the
Colour and number of petals,
Sniff and approve the aroma
And extend my hand towards
Your presence? I am fairly tall,
Negligibly handsome and could
Speak with my eyes. Will my
Offering taunting a definition
Encircle your vision, ever?

That's why all these well-read love stories
Hatched in public transports
And morphed inside kundera's
Novel never belong to us. Now please
Stop and do not ask poor me to replicate
Any of the stories ever.

Dreams

Beautiful dreams mostly shed
Their colours with hungry promises.
We word our departure,
The last butterfly breaks its rampant
Wings seeking a direction,
Never painted.

Why is it so dark when we
Seek our needy fingers
Clasping in mutual enchantment? The
Room has a design, a destiny,
But no space for our
Togetherness!

You go. Go with the knowledge
That my desire follows you
Blindfolded. My desire has
Hundred tongues, a burnishing fire
And no eyes. You touch, I
Reinstate my hunger. You desist,
I fall into the darkness
Of our making, songless.

Now my dreams have your
Absence tangled into
Lovely frames. Each frame has
A collage and each assemblage
A motto of cursed silence. Do
Give a caption to my love
Even if you design my fall,
I know all seasons must die
And my love must also suffer.

Acknowledging Loss

I acknowledge. It is
Not mine to give,
This speechless donation
Of private dreams. Dreams
Have sudden endings,
They always sprout on the
Principle of daily living, like the
One way passage seeking your
Bodyless presence.

You belong to all the
Ricocheted attraction converted
Into love. The message must remain
Hidden, encrypted in
Unfulfilled desire and
An ageless hurt.

Still I have to sing, these
Songs are my salvaged
Daily wear. I have to paint,
All primitive colours are
Tinted with my amaranthine waiting.
Some lines may touch your heart
And flower in the canvas
Of impure magic. You will be somewhere
Encashing enchantment.

I confess, it is never in my
Control to not to
Wake up in the middle of the
Night, under a touch
Of unseen aroma and feel
Your absence seized by
Hungry sighs and shrouded by
Dead memories.

Intimacy

Do not cross the
Threshold.
Darkness has fanged
Embrace, silence
As eyes.
Your body will melt
In hunger, walls
Salivate in impatience.

Do not surrender to
The entrance, the doors
Lead to ancient world of
Bones sizzling in lust.
Love lurks somewhere, wait
And seek the moonlight
Outside. Then count the
Steps that you reach out in
Softly and drench you in
The first rain of acceptance.

Open the doors
And switch on the lamps.
Hunger is lit now
On syllables of togetherness,
Our bodies next to the burning candle.

Left Behind

You left me under
Shining clouds
Devouring rain. I stood
By the footpath confused
Inside strange murmurs
Haloing the moving crowd
You did not look back
When a small crack appeared
As a loss never to be
Mended again and will open as
A protected wound bleeding
In sighs.

Our days probably had magic
Of their own, our being together.
Love caught us unphotographing
In smoke filled bars, cafes,
Pretending to be tree laden paintings,
Inside a hotel room and in
Our shared physicality of belonging.
Our days probably had to end like
All magic assassinated by reality
Lurking around our weak bones,
Nourishing dreams and hungry Lives.

You could have waited a bit
Longer. Shadows could have consoled
Me and assembled my lonesome fall
Into a single waiting. You just
Left. A gigantic sky of benign
Melancholia now lives beside me
In my drinks, in my dreams, in my poetry and in your absence.

Falling Down

This body falls
Like drops of melting wax
From a burning candle
Of swelling desire. Your
Touches reach niches
Of non-existent inners
In hardening flesh and
Thirsty bones. Mist of your
Embrace envelops a sky
Inside the clouds of blinking desire and
I surrender.

Our lovemaking has wordless
Etudes, pictures of hoary
Togetherness. You call amid a
Stampede of caressing sighs and I reply
With a belly full of
Wild fluttering dragonflies.We create
Moments of ancient magic, with
Enchantment in trance.

Can we preserve the essence
Of our feel and touch, rustle
Of our thighs and the forest of
This bodily cacophonies inside our
Capsuled now? I wish I knew, but
I recognise the insatiable
Prayers that resonate in our
Togetherness and we celebrate.

Enchantment

These steps have fluidity, but
They painfully cramp. One never
Knows how silence covers up
A world of personal symphony, so
Easily, yet has all the music to sustain
Movements. Of hunger and brutal
Melancholia!

We all master the art of sinful
Begging. We beg for love, purity of
Togetherness, a season of rare
Aroma and never for the punishing
Distance that haunts dreams
And sleeplessness.

I fall. Always the charm has
Devoted colours. Your face
Simulates identity and my
Prayers. In this life all psalms
Are sung in deceptive
Minors. I lose. You pretend
A placement sewn in our
Love you disown.

The style is all mine now. The
Choreography of waiting
Will combine with our lost
Melodies, dead songs, craving
For words and my lonesome
Destiny for your going away
Unnoticed.
I must keep on dancing, the
Steps may become faulty. You know.
Yet your recognition will remain so far
Away in my cursed darkness of
Constantly missing you.

Understanding Loss

Eternity flutters on the estuary
Of still waters and flickering sunlight.
Atop a broken mirage of a mirror, the
Image procures dignity of
Evaporating silence. A song
Stings, meaningless words crowd
And envelope the face, then it
Transforms into a wardrobe of daily
Living. Dreams shatter, to be
Arranged in a promise of a
Tomorrow, unironed.

I could always stand beside the
Carrousel of broken relations. The
Faces are half devoured by the
Charted distances, relations corroded
By acid of untamed time. But
The sound have the weight to touch
My graphic uncertainties. I remember
And I keep on living on the throbs of
Many natural demises and few natural rebirths.

I am the mirror, the broken shards of
The lining of undigested light, and
Hints of shadows yet to find
Addresses and identities. Before the
Picture discloses itself inside a
Bonsai treachery of curtailed
Realisation, a prayer beckons,
Mostly as death, but also
The lilting song of being with
You, in my devotion to life
That I fear to understand.

Letting Go

This book of love poems is not mine. Page
57 line 15 still blames me for abandoning my

Desire for you in favour of unattainable
Love. The feather marking the agony parched

Words is dusty, belongs to a migratory species.
That bird must have covered a whole lot of

Distance and the lonely Sky! I sometimes
Caress the margins for lost memories. Your

Love for poetry does not echo anymore
Inside my empty ribs, filled only with songs

And a silence devoted to my living. One's own
Shadow dictates the sadness of a hazy

Past. I had left you then with reluctant
Footsteps riding tensile hunger of
Unfulfilment.

You did not utter a word. This book of
Love poems now vomit all such words and emotions.

Overpowering my distance. The dedication is all
About living, never ascribed to our love, love

Cannot be death of desire foretold.

Breaking Patterns

Inside the circle of misunderstood
Relations, I hurt easily. Outside, I hurt
People. I live by tempting imagination and
Love with captive desire. Desires keeps
Me starved. The famine of the hungry body
Is not where emotions grow, temptation
Glows. Hunger always rules, I just
Survive.

Why can not I reconstruct what I
Lack in love, with borrowed pictures
Of attraction and implant understanding?
Love must one day clean my wounds,
Touch my scarred lips and wash away
My definable amnesia. Then how come
Everyone around my night of uncontrollable
Exile gape at the vacant moonlight promising
Salvation prescribed against my waiting,
For you! Yet I prefer to
Suffer in ignorance. Without you.

I really need you. Need expressed
Blatantly in love, desire, lust and
Desperation. But I cannot promise
The pain I impose myself in giving
And the sorrow I unconditionally
Borrow from you in blood and flesh.
I know I will hurt you. I have
To love and live in such distress,
All my life in my way.

Dying Lotuses

You do not have to weep over the
Dying lotuses. The water level is again
Almost right to sprout new

Dreams. You can see the Images of the
Trees,the sky, all the dots to be calculated as
Flying birds and your darkness in

The waveless surface. If you start
Crying, your tears will not have to the
Power a torrential raindrop carries.

They will mostly plop arousing self-pity
And disappoint. You must know, all these
Flowers charming the water bed with

Managed memories carry history and
Hurt all with predetermined prophecy of
Those which must die and become folklore.

Imagined stories weaves at in dreams
And never construct daily rituals for persons
Scared of water in all seasons.

Commuting Loss

A dead Moon was floating
On the bed of disfigured clouds.
It was yet dark with unknown
Shadows crying inside silhouette of
Distant trees. Breathless flickering of
Unwanted time was begging for the
Hurried feet to cross the threshold
Of mutant dreams, stunted waiting
And a moonless midnight.

Every night storms the captive space
Heart can not define nor relationship
Could defend. A blanket of melancholia
Invites the eyes of the dark to shed
Memories and cherish tears. Every night
Is another reproduction of the aroma spent,
Restlessness awaken amid the Lost
Prayers of all wantings not yet sated.

It was one such night when we all lost our
Virgin dreams. Now our personal world
Detains a full moon night populated in
Mute memories, love being the daily ritual inside
The crowd of weeping shadows.

Remaining Words

These are petrified
Words,
Hung limp and punctured
From shivering lips
Dead with cold messages.
Many discarded heartbeats
Lie next to crowded
Waitings. These words now
Do not carry
Wings fluttering with dreams
Nor any hope to soar
In love. They are also barred to
Touch the burning warmth
Oozing from the fresh skin
And enchant on their own.
These words are rinsed
In ancient curses, nurturing
Rejection, lonesome hunger and
Wanton distances. One just can
Not get rid of
Their allure nor can throw them off
As discarded feelings.
They are there
Like melted Moonlight crisscrossing
The empty room and never locating dear darkness
Hiding in the corner.

We have to live with these
Remaining words, hoping for
An opening that may appear as
Silent betrayal or maybe as
Love never foretold.

Picture Imperfect

All the catalogued pictures, familiar to
Me from the days of the marigold sunset
And sandy river bed, refuse to

Return to this cannabis indicted
Exile, to this drunken despair with
No meanings. I continue to fumble for

The Lost words, seek them in any opened
Eyes, non-readable lips and unheard of
Distances. Sometimes they torture the living,

Raise a forest of self doubt and
Keep all the prefabricated anguish at a
Safe address hidden from the personal moorings

Easily lost. Yet the floodgate of blind
Waiting incessantly tempt. In the hope
That these unmolested timid words could

Open the pores of tired denials, touch the
Sleepless eyelids and start humming the
Most simple songs eluding me for eons.

A Prayer

Please pray for me.
Tattered scabs of cruel
Darkness almost
Cover my whole body, my naked
Soul shivers outside.
I live in a house of darkness,
The walls crumble with
Ancient sins, with odour
Of uninvited curses.

Touch my forehead with
Any truth that speaks
Of light, of atonement.
Then wash my existence
In teardrops and faith,
And give me an embrace,
Of rekindling dignity
And for seeking.

Please lay down a tatami
Of serrated light, I
Have to shed my shadows
And cry for a new beginning.
I have to commence
This journey of
Awakening for my redemption,
Love beckons.

This Night

It will rain dead music
Whole night. Flickering
Sparks of a buried moon
Will litter the sky amid
Unwanted clouds.

The only song,
Which could caress my
Lips with wordless abandon and
With my eyes spitting
Prohibited desire,
Will ease off from this
Cursed orbit with your
Departure. I can only
Witness as predetermined, but
Without a personal text.

I carry the tote bag of
Charmed curses. Love will hunt
And hurt me, your going away
Will curate a world of lonesome
Dignity lapping my sorrows and
Always waiting will cartograph a
Destiny, never mine but
Must be kept corralled in this
Lifetime.

It will bleed dark memories
Whole night. I cannot die nor
Can I cry in hiding. The night
Must carry me into the shadows
Of indistinct suffering tattooed in
Eons of absence of your making.

Conveying an Absence

Every time I translate the
Phalanx of unmade colours into
Shod messages of love, you
Disappear. Your Absence adds
Vigour to pain and a season of
Dreamy waiting. A surreal
Light, you donated and I did not see,
Hovers over my days. Then I
Lose all meanings there and then and survive.

Survival is the theme of my pictorial
Distance. Far I step away from
The rain soaked mud of your
Lost footprint, shadows crowd me
Like wounded prayers. They return
Me to my world of cages, echoing
Whispers and detained sighs.

But I am a mere translator of
Captive distortions. Love Enchants
Me and kills. Simple words of
Your recognition revives me into
This world of hung pictures, each
Picture depicting my destiny for hurting over and over again.

Tracing Return

I have to call off the wake and walk.
Initially my feet will drag on the muddy
Directionlessness, then the sad songs will
Converge like hundreds of ink coloured
Birds flapping inside a glass attic. I
Will not have any possessed time to
Remember the teardrops that did not turn
Into pearls of hungry memory. Nor will
I have broken fragments of pet
Dreams to recall lost enchantment
With a name, few dates and your face.

Everything we create has to be slayed by the
Ferocity of love returned, heart sullied by
The aeronautics of private betrayal and
Togetherness stored atop the mantle of a hurt mind with
Cursed incurable silence. Everything. Then all
I can do is to wait, discard meaningless
Pain and start the budding steps. These steps
Must have some essence of looking back and
Regenerate waiting, must have some dignity
In shedding tears and flowers into another
Strange destiny, away from you and towards love.

Catchphrases

I will never seek you again
Inside the labyrinth of hurt
Shadows. I lose my way, faces
Alter relationship, hunger rules.
Losing you is never living,
I have to begin again and again.

You will come, come with the
Dancing stream of verdant
Recognition. Your steps will
Streak into haloing lines
Of pure love. I will obviously
Be prepared, yet stunned
By the grace and power of your
Arrival on the sharpened
Hour blades of our togetherness.

I promise, I will not chase after
Unfamiliar dreams, courting
Mirage, trying to catch
Your presence in a crowd of
Unsold attractions.

Just a murmur is enough. When
It is your time to irrigate my
Parched heart, your love
Will jump from the threshold
Of my waiting personal sky
Till it breaks the silence spread
Into our music of vibrant
Raindrops,
Enveloping us in the clouds
Of finding each other every time, here and now.

Notebook Lines

Draw a circle please.
Before I step inside, do
Construct an arc of
Unmade assurances.

See how I totter
With anticipation. This body
Of shredded disguise
Has to find a foothold.
In the island of sheer
Acceptance. You have
To be around somewhere.

Then you paint the pictures.
The tree branches whispering with
The wind, a naive cloud flying in
Autumn abandon, we are to
Discover lifesize togetherness
Or a forest of waiting vibrating in
Wordlessness.

We are inside the circle, woman,
Each step has its own calling,
If in the name of love, we dance
With drunken steps, if in despair,
Our songs die before I read
The message without your mute declarations.

For You

I can only deal with
Controlled words from a
Distance, real world
Scares me like imaginary
Raw wounds that
Never heal, bleed on their own.

You always fashion a beautiful
Dress of happiness, coloured
Feminine sparkles in your eyes.
You speak and hum of
Enchanting my life, abuzz with
Lovely beginning and togetherness.
Your aroma Pervades my personal history
And promises in giving. Your
Smile liberates my love to its
Purest form. You give so much
Yet reach out and touch my melting
Core of eternal hunger in abundant intimacy.

I melt, I stumble, I fall,
You extend your arms,
You shimmer,
I grope like the falling star, in
Waiting darkness of your
Inviting body, seeping your love,
Wanting more. Let me break
Into flowering dreams of
Our seeking this lifetime
To belong, with you.

Missing

Can not string a touch of
Intense desire here, this is the
Framed anguish of moonlight nights
And a hovering cloud, aloof and hungry.

I pass my time here in the backyard of
Designed routine. My shadows wither
And all the doorways carry the same
Messages painted by hollering darkness. But I
Cannot leave before a season of dead
Flowers bedeck this body
With promiselessness.

You have to know. Somewhere inside the
Empty circle of impure heartbeats
Awaiting catches fire. You never
See how it rains for countless days
And one night before a limp rainbow
Climbs on my soul and sends me back
To my room filled with negatives
Of losses, never to be developed in this life.

A Blurred Picture

Across the window the float of
Swirling rain hangs over the
Hungry trees. Distance shimmers in
Hazy light, wind pauses.

Rain reminds me of your appearing
Inside a territory of my desire. You
Came donating a semi-formed rainbow
Echoing love, you decorated the
Windows of hunger in trickling
Raindrops, I drank in enchantment.

You also left when the rain poured into
The bed of disagreement we kept
Unprepared. Thunder hid my hurt, you
Disappeared with the blades of lightning
Without a caring glance. It rained
For many nights, enveloped a whole
Existence in unwanted sorrow.

Now always rain will tiptoe with your
Fragile aroma, will caress poetry and
Pity in autumnal footsteps. I will
Devote whole pages of our togetherness in
Singing for rain that once drenched me with happiness
Shrouded in your blurred pictures.

Distance

Ask me a simple question,
Only one permitted in this
Lifetime.
If it is just about love,
I will plead for therapeutic
Silence to seal my lips
And whisper awkwardness.

If you fail to ask,
It remains still the world of
Soporific music, starting
From my enchanted throat
And empowering my nothingness.
I sing and I Dance.
Yet the fences between us
Stand invisible and weak.

Now a days
I seek you without words,
And I wait for your
Presence overriding my doubts
That you mostly exist in my
Imagination.

Any Moment

A capsule of blue hurt
Could so easily consume all the
Time we had spent together, I could
Never imagine. You did
Not stop to look back, to see
The folded pile of dead strands,
That was our enchantment,
Also our seeking nuances of so
Much love and hunger, body and
Beauty of shared fragrance,
Ambushed me, all alone and forlorn.

Now your absence is an entity
Of diverse pain. I kill my
Lonely moments on a cross
Of distances, between my ancient
Dreams you had coloured and my
Cruel days of transition,
Hurt devours.

I will not call you again with
The voice at the midnight train,
I will not tango my surrender
Again with the steps of
Your beckoning. Of course I
Will bear the tattoos of your
Naked body stamping my
Painted desire, all the time, in
Summer rain and winter leaflessness

I carry the coin of closing
My séance of love this time.
One side is what you gave in
Wonderful relationship and
Other side is my loss, tampered
In pure hurt. I can never
Spend this coin in this lifetime,
Even if memory announces the
Closure of the market of your absence on any loveless day!

In Exile

Let me go. I have to step out
And carve a passable distance
Inside the forest of strange shadows.

This shadow has fierce hunger but
No fangs. Fear is a halo around my
Naked dreams. I must not be afraid

Till you again open the door on your own for my
Orphan songs of desire to seek
The ledge and your invitation back to the season

Of togetherness in love. Let me go. I also
Have to seek love inside the
Exile of many lives and a single

Betrayal. Everything must appear as a
Perfect routine where always I have to
Leave and never to return to your world on my own.

Emoting Loss

Not a line was written about losing you. Not a
Word had splintered into vicious memory bytes to
Let you go

But the planchette of despair had forecasted
About blood and flesh conspiring together, tear and
Sadness oozing into lonesome manhood's seeking
Insufficient answers.

All meanings construct their own escape routes,
Life unbundles its own reflections. Remaining
Spaces, while tumbleweed outside the front door of
Bearable existence, comprise of lost love and
Mythical memories.

Nowadays I do not sing anymore lores of
Enchantment you had taught me. I just pass
My expired time struggling to overcome an
Aroma that still tortures my soul without your
Being there in any form of a seasonal flower.

Songs That Refuse To Die

Just a simple weaver of discounted
Words, I fail often. The tunes I
Embed in my existence of impure
Struggle return to me incomplete
Without your acceptance.

It is true that the songs which
Scour the primitive dreams of
Mine like your old wounds
Decently healed, your scars that
Only memorize pain as ungainly history.
I know my words remain
Mute, unfulfilled and tame,
Ricocheting from the walls of
Simple rejection you erect.

These songs carry hunger, echo
Love and fester in immense
Waiting. My voice carries imprints
Of unscaled time begging for
Space you will provide. Nobody
Knows when the concert of lonely
Pebbles will magically float in waves
Of your recognition. They forgot to die.

Answering For Nothing

Ask me a simple question. I
Will seek the sparkles in your
Eyes and lose all my humming words.

Our love is like that. We catch
Moments in our beckoning and
Build gossamer dreams. The tune
Flutters in our togetherness.

I borrow pure pleasure from your
Unreachable durability. You give
My petrified hunger a
Season of filtering beauty, my love
Candle drops your recognition. I
Breathe and belong.

I can not imagine hurting a day
Without your donating
Tender echoes practicing possession inside
My heart. You are and I exist fulfilled
On the collage of your lips, sighs, body
And desire.

I will answer one day. Under the
Appliqué colours of our enchantment,
I will dedicate a painting, heart shaped.

Any Name

Ask
Each counting
Fermenting from
Tear drops
And bleeding

Life is not
So sanguine
Our compromises
Kill our
Aroma and
Produce selfies for
Our losses, we
Always loose.

Why is it so
Painful to inherit
Your own hunger
Before the
Desire's web sells
You to others?
Do not pretend, this body
Rebuilds images and
You design your
Absence for nothing.

Now bones elevate
Music of waiting in
Hundreds of lost names.
I confess, hardly a name
Is known to me, in
Love and in seeking.

Leaving

I have no option
But to leave

The door ajar.

Wind has enough
Fluency to
Carry all the dead
Messages and hang
A battered blue kite
Below the highest branches
That heart can pretend to receive as a tree

Waiting will be emoting
Consolation outside.

I now never sleep inside
The camera of self-belief.
Outside life tortures

Inside the house, I paint
Canvases, devoid of Love.

Homecoming : an Odisha Poem

A lonely tide
Soaking forms
Over spotless sands,
Often wipes away
My footprints. I
Have to seek direction
Again. The roaring
Sea eats up words
Pointing homeward
And I must reach
Home before a single
Strand silver moon is
Shadowed in darkness.

Many years now, this
Ritual mirrors faces
Long gone, relatives
Long dead. Familiar
Sounds from home and
Temples, slums and suburbs
Now rehearse
Unknown addresses. Death
And distances hovers in
Alien photographs. I must
Arrive in front of the only
Door step that pretends
In waiting anytime my
Sighs eat up my identity
And I am home.

This is the friend who

Threw love into
Kamikaze betrayal. That
Woman gave herself
In false promises which
Corroded Love. The
Traffic still crawls into
Daily banalities. I have
Stopped seeking my
Brokered fame in my hometown.
All are my friends and
My lovers. I return to
Wash the stripped ribbon
Around my soul
In memory soap, so rare.

Till I wear the
Faithless curse etched
In exile, I will return
Again and again. I will
Take off my mask and
Look again towards distinct
Losses and bundled memories.
Hope I have not forgotten
My glasses behind, life tends
To go blind lately.

Translating Loss

By the time nocuous pain hurt my tears,
Distance was the colour of the sari you
Were wearing. I fell.

Probably you did not wait to see how my
Uncharted dreams ransacked my haunted
Desires. I could not save anything from

A hung over past, love counting irate
Butterflies inside a terrified heart, hunger
Mounting a distinct parade for your

Naked body inside my unpatented
Loss. Neither could I paint an empty
Canvas for recouping personal history, of
Our togetherness,

Just I fell. I have to get up on my own,
Lying around vacant shadows scared me.
Now I have to tend to this growing forest

In bodily waiting. Waiting reminds me of
Words unsaid and on its bare wall
Hangs your picture wearing spaceless

Betrayal and my naked despair.

In Love

Give me your love, love is
Like pre recuperative oxygen its
need undocumented.

But do not ever permit me to preach
Substance in return. I flourish
in what you give, but I stay in a
World of self-doubt, often populated
By an unimaginative itch.

I can be any man yet I am no one's
Man. Your touch feeds my
Heart, your body unhinges all
My nebulous waiting and you
Open up all my unseen pores
Of angst into becoming a shape of your translucent love.
Can you retain me like this!

Do not unfetter all my animal wounds,
My hunger untames shadows. They
Always take me away from your
Love and from myself. Then when
The emptiness of roaring melancholia
Paws my chest and mauls my
Eyelids, l fail to recognise you
And I am irretrievablylost,
Just inches outside your love, away
From the protection of your being there.

This Book

This book must be sold
With numbered pages.

Each page must offer a
Believable storyline playing
Silent séance with written words.

We always agree to discount
The frivolous readership. Books
Have their own musty aroma to flourish.

This book covets pictures that
Hold life's difficulties in happy
Bibliography. Does ownership crowd the

Book in love and distances? I will not
Know. This book is a heirloom of untold
Images, varied emotions, but must be sold.

The peaks that touch
And pierce the roofs.
From the upthrusting
Of the continents,
To the trenches
Of the crushing depths,
None equal the hill of Sisyphus.

All must labor up
With the boulder
That will bury them—

No matter what,
Their greatness or their fame—
With the tombstone
Of their inextricable triumph
And shame.

Nirala Series

A Series of Contemporary Writing

Kailash: Jewel of the Snows
Rajinder Arora
ISBN: 978-8193936719 Paperback 2021 pp 268
plus 68 color Demy

A Short History of Nepal
From Ancient to Modern Times
Shreeram Prasad Upadhyaya
ISBN 9-788182-500174 2021 PP 255

Mother's Hand: Selected Poems
A Bilingual English/Nepali Anthology
by **Jidi Majia**
Translated into Nepali by **Yuyutsu RD Sharma**
ISBN: 978-8182500174 Paperback pp 96 Demy

Dancing in Place: *New Poems*
S. Renay Sanders
ISBN ISBN 81-8250-048-6 2019 pp. 64 Paper Demy

Blue Fan Whirring: *Poems*
Mike Jurkovic
ISBN 978-8182500969 2019 pp. 160 Paper

The Second Buddha Walk:
Inspired by The Second Buddha ,
Master of Time Exhibit at Rubin Museum, New York
Yuyutsu Sharma
ISBN 978-8182500983 2019 pp. 52 Paper Demy

Imagined Secrets: *New Poems*
Robert Scotto
ISBN 978-81825000442019 pp. 79 Paper Demy

The Tin Man
David B. Austell
ISBN 9-788182-500792 2019 pp.320 Hard Demy

All Vows: : *New & Selected Poems*
David B. Axelrod
ISBN 978-8182500822 2016 pp 194

The Dhimals: Miraculous Migrants of Himal:
An Anthropological Study of a Nepalese Ethnic Group
Rishikeshab Raj Regmi
ISBN 9788182500082 2016 PP 294

Path to Excellence: : *A Memoir by India's Distinguished Academician*
Pritam B. Sharma
ISBN : 81-8250-0907 2017 Hard Cover pp 358

Word Has It, Poems
Ruth Danon
ISBN 81-8250-097-4 2018 Paperback pp 85

Eternal Snow: *A Worldwide Anthology of One Hundred Twenty Five Poetic Intersections with Himalayan Poet Yuyutsu RD Sharma*
Edited by **David Austell & Kathleen D Gallagher**
ISBN : 81-8250-088-5 2017 Paperback pp 309

Cats, Love & Other Surprises
by **Otis Kidwell Burger**, Illustrations by Katherine Burger
ISBN : 978-8182500891 2017 Hardback pp 65 RS. 1495

Letters from a Sacred Mountain Place:
A Journey through the Nepal Himalayas –
Photographs and Text by **Diane Frank**
ISBN 81-8250-095-8 2018 Hard Cover pp 144

Making of The Indian Muse
Context and Perspectives in Indian Poetry in English
Edited by **Goutam Karmakar**
ISBN 978-8182500273 2019 pp 430

Ritual: The Magical Perspective : *Efficacy an the Search for Inner Meaning*
Luc Sala
ISBN 9-788182-500617 2014 Hard pp.832

A Blizzard In My Bones: New York Poems
Yuyutsu RD Sharma
ISBN 81-8250-070-2 2016 pp.134 Paper

Inside the Shell of the Tortoise
Poems written in India and Nepal : ***A Spanish English Edition***
Veronica Aranda
Translated by **Claudia Routon** with **Yuyutsu Sharma**
ISBN 9-788182-500686 2016 pp.56 Hard

Your Kiss is a River : *Poems of Love, Food and Life*
Carolyn Wells
ISBN 9-788182-500532 2016 pp.56 Hard

Space Cake, Amsterdam
& Other Poems from Europe and America
Yuyutsu RD Sharma
ISBN-81-8250-059-1 2014 Hard pp. 110

Milarepa's Bones, Helambu : *33 New Poems*
Yuyutsu RD Sharma
ISBN-81-8250-032-X 2012 Hard pp.64

Little Creek *& Other Poems*
David Austell
ISBN 81-8250- 031-1 2011 Hard pp.200

The Mystery Over Lord Buddha's Roots
An Analysis of the Mystery of the Shakya Kingdom
Mitsuaki KOJIMA
ISBN 9-788182-500563 2014 Hard pp.165

TEN: The New Indian Poets
Selected and Edited by **Jayanta Mahapatra & Yuyutsu Sharma**
ISBN 9-788182-500341 2012 pp.134 Hard

Dada Poetry :*An Introduction* by **William Seaton**
Foreword by **Timothy Shipe**
ISBN-9-788182-500358 2013 Hard pp.112

Libraries, Information Centers &
Information Professionalism in Nepal by Madhusudan Karki
ISBN 9-788182-500372 2012 Hard pp.348

The Yeti : **Spirit of Himalayan Forest Shamans by Larry G. Peters**
ISBN 9-788182-500525 2014 Hard pp.128

Folk Tales of Sherpa and Yeti
Collected by **Shiva Dhakal**, *Adapted by* **Yuyutsu RD Sharma**
ISBN 9-788182-500624 2014 Paper pp.125

Annapurnas & Stains of Blood:*Life, Travel & Writing on a page of Snow*
Yuyutsu RD Sharma
ISBN 9-788182-500129 2010 Hard pp.200

Trance, Initiation & Psychotherapy in Nepalese Shamanism
Essays on Tamang and Tibetan Shamanism by **Larry G. Peters**
ISBN 9-788182-500532 2014 Paper pp.412

Tamang Shamans :
An Ethnopsychiatric Study of Ecstasy and Healing in Nepal
Larry G. Peters ISBN 9-788182-500099 2007 Paper pp.179

The Pokhara Valley : *A Traveler's Guide by* **LB Thapa**
ISBN 9-788182-500198 2010 Paper pp.202

Ocean in a Drop: *Yoga, Meditation and Life in the Himalayas*
Swami Chandresh
ISBN 81-8250- 005-2 2006 Hard pp.348

The Price of Heaven *Travel Stories from India and Nepal*
Evald Flisar
Translated from Slovene by **the Author & Alan McConnell-Duff**
ISBN 81-8250- 020-6 2009 Paper pp.140

Student Politics & Democracy in Nepal by Meena Ojha
ISBN 9-788182-500259 2010 Hard pp.411

WHITE LOTUS BOOKS

I Choose to Cry and Love You:
Maile Roje Runa Ra Timilai Maya Garna
(A Bilingual English/Nepali)
Yang Qingxiang Translated into the Nepali by Yuyutsu Sharma
ISBN: 978-9937079013 Paperback 2021 pp355 Dem

Ek Asadharan Antarvarta: Flash Fiction
by Lao Ma Translated into Nepali by Yuyutsu Sharma
ISBN: 978-9937-0-7902-0 Paperback 2021 pp 334 Demy

Panaharu Khalichan : Kavitaka Dui Dashak (Poems)
Yuyustu R.D. Sharma
ISBN 81-8250-004-4 2020 Paper pp. 140

Bhojpure Hulakiko Santaan, Atamgat (A Memoir)
Shailendra Sakar ISBN: 978-9937056526 Paperback 2021 pp 209 Demy

Nachganko Rajdhani Bhaktapur:
(Bhaktapur A City of Music & Dance)
Jagadish Rana ISBN 978-8182500433 Hardcover 2011 pp 84

Nirdoshharuko Nyaya ra anya Kavitaharu by David B. Austell
ISBN 9789937056533 pp.40 2015 Paperback

EPSILONMEDIA BOOKS

Annapurna, Everest, Helambu & Langtang : Mini Nepal Trilogy
Poetry by Yuyutsu RD Sharma, *Photographs* by Andreas Stimm
ISBN: 978-3981088342 Hardcover 2015 pp 200

The Nepal Trilogy Part I-III Annapurna, Everest,
Helambu & Langtang
Hasselblad XPan photographs & Poetryfrom the main trekking areas of Nepal. www.Nepal-Trilogy.de,
English-german ISBN: ISBN 978-3-9810883-2-8)
Paperback Box 2015 pp 800